The Occupant

poems by

Patricia Murphy

Finishing Line Press
Georgetown, Kentucky

The Occupant

For my husband Daryl Lee who sees something in me and loves me. For Alicia Billman and Catherine Billman, my first true loves. For Lena Bertone whose heart and hugs are monumental.

Copyright © 2017 by Patricia Murphy
ISBN 978-1-63534-147-8 First Edition
All rights reserved under International and Pan-American Copyright Conventions. No part of this book may be reproduced in any manner whatsoever without written permission from the publisher, except in the case of brief quotations embodied in critical articles and reviews.

ACKNOWLEDGMENTS

CityArt: "Under Water"
Arsenic Lobster, Second Serving: "The Life of the Shepherd"
River Walk Literary Journal: "Zoology"
Breadcrumb Scabs: "The Story of Us," "homewreck," "Winterish" and "Not on My Life"
Yes, Poetry: "This is not a poem about Icarus" and "Alien, My Love Monster"
Adagio Verse: Moment of Truth"

Publisher: Leah Maines

Editor: Christen Kincaid

Cover Art: Daryl Lee

Author Photo: Daryl Lee

Cover Design: Elizabeth Maines McCleavy

Printed in the USA on acid-free paper.
Order online: www.finishinglinepress.com
also available on amazon.com

Author inquiries and mail orders:
Finishing Line Press
P. O. Box 1626
Georgetown, Kentucky 40324
U. S. A.

Table of Contents

Heart

Personal History 1
homewreck 2
Under Water 3
Buying Wood for Winter 4
Alien, My Love Monster 5
Zoology 6
Optical Illusion 7
The Occupant 8
Some Thoughts on the Problem of Solitude 9

Head

Moment of Truth 10
Poem for John Ashbery and Michael Burkard 11
Ginsberg and Eliot Look Down on Robert Hass Reading
    "Privilege of Being" 12
This Is Not a Poem about Icarus 13
Staring Contest: For Herodotus 14
The Highway Girl 15
The Capital of Me 16

Home

Five Years On: Clinton, NY 2008 17
English Teacher 18
On the E Train 20
Earthquake 21
Saratoga Springs in the Off-season 22
Bird Watching In Central New York 24
On Vacation in Cape Cod I think of Idaho, Home, and
    Other Places 26
We All Go A'looking 27
One Morning 28
Leaving Idaho Behind 29
Winterish 30
Not on My Life 31
When I Went Back To Idaho—For Catherine 32
Springtime in Central New York 33

Heart

Personal History

Yes, I will pull you under water.
But not the cool slick time you
Imagine in the back of your eye.

No, you will not think of sidewalks
Any more than you did in the glycerin night
When they were building trains again

And the mouths of furnaces opened up
On the western edge of town
In a land of industrial darkness.

Yes, we are both gone to foothills
With no mountains behind them
And lakes with kerosene edges.

Our history isn't all frayed boundaries,
Your story anxious as a time of drought
Waiting for my oily fingers to return.
Our story isn't lit by just one lamp

Heart

homewreck

it's easy to imagine your body as a place   as cartography with swirls for small mountains and landscapes that can tumble and metaphor   it's easy to imagine your body as a house I want to occupy   a window I can climb through   an open door with want and need its threshold   I don't define you through the lens of words enough   I know you are all abrasion and rift sometimes and clanking door too   I don't want what I want when I know what I want   I can't lie as if a lily on a pond   that's just not me   I'm all poltergeist of words and thoughts the thing that scurries across the roof in the middle of the night   I've never taken the real way out   I've never really known   inside   I think sometimes my tongue is waiting for a paper cut

the way that razors wait to be put into door frames   the way that fire waits to fill up a house   the way that time waits to cut up all my endeavors   I'm in dog time howling at the infected eyes of cheap grocery store bouquets   you're a dream experienced in stages:

    one is when I close my eyes

two, when I open them a little

                    and in the third dream you're a little past the long cold tunnel   that connects two parts of the same town

Here is a word I mispronounced once at a time when pronunciation mattered: apotheosis
Here is a time I wanted nothing and felt no greed: last Saturday
Here is the thing I wish I'd never touched: velvet
Here is the sound I love:

Under Water

When I was a child I was afraid to swim in natural water.
I feared the dead were there, waiting to pull me under.
As a child I was afraid to look under bushes—
in the undergrowth the dead might lie waiting.
When I was a child mirrors were places where I
might see them in side glances, looking back at me.

Often, I dreamed of old men walking with stones in their hands,
shuffling toward altars that had no saint names,
stones that shone light from older calendars—their singular burden.
In shadows changed by cloud-travel, optical illusions occur.
Under water shaped by the passage of swimming bodies,
we see ghosts where there is really only seaweed.

Now I sit under skies that beg poems and refuse ambiguity.
Clouds like chessmen and starfish drift toward their finish line.

Some days, this sky is the blue of your eyes, both impossible to represent
in ink.
These days the living occupy my time since I have become one of them.

Heart

Buying Wood for Winter

We drive down the highway
on the first cold day in autumn, and
the air is hazy, the land tan.
On one side of the road by a butte
(a glorified gopher mound) a beet dump steams
round and squatty, fermenting pre-sugar,
massive lumps sitting passively
waiting to be converted.

But they resist and stare back blank,
unsorted, expressionless, and bland,
not distinguished from their companions
by any apparent landmarks. They are not
scenic and they keep me out.
They don't turn into a woman's
back, or ship hulls. They don't seem like
loaves of bread, steam irons, or anybody's nipple.

The wood smells—woody, and the day gets hotter
as we work side by side.
My mind imagines us pre-lapsarian,
in the days before we fell into a
middle-aged syncopation orchestrated
by children, jobs, aging parents and
this need to define ourselves by our
responsibilities, to feel industrious and worthy.

This fall I fell headlong
from the tree of all I'd planned on,
and when I landed on the ground I couldn't
regain my footing. My markers were gone.
The descent was fast and furious and it left me sick from the change
in altitude,
deflated, and suddenly aware that I had something to fall from.

Heart

Alien, My Love Monster

Far away you dream my belly
The one with the line down the middle
Through which babies came sprawling into the world.
The one you've neither seen nor touched

Years ago I went to New York in spring
And bought you a book, first edition,
Signed by a poet you loved and emulated.
Your lines like his held out only so much
Until restraint took over.

Secrets back in the box, yours, his, mine—
The book my small offering to what you wanted
As March took over from the longest winter of our lives.

Now we walk such different streets, you and I.
My drum is syncopated to the only rhythm I know,
Yours to everyone else's.
I like my drum better than yours.

Now, when the sky streaks toward the West with cold pink fingers
Pointing "come home," I think of you and the book I put away.

Heart

Zoology

Your hands are silverfish
circling and erudite
concentric and articulate.

At night when
you pet the cat
I want to be the cat
and when
you talk to the cat in purrs
I want to be the cat
and when
the cat rubs against you
trusting you
I want to be
the cat.

Heart

Optical Illusion
    When it's the wine talking you know you'd better listen.

A man sits next to me at a bar. He could be uglier,
But it's hard to see how. His face is all tremulous craters,
Caked maybe by the absence of good hygiene.
But the more I drink, the more he makes sense,
Becomes beautiful with the soul of a poet.

Rich and languid,
His words sail up with the cigarette smoke. We're in a bar
That hasn't fallen prey to smoking bans, or one where the bartender
Hides the ashtray when someone he doesn't know comes in.
This man, he's seen it all, he's done it all, he knows all the places
In the desert where the stars are so big they give you eye sores.
He says eye sores, really he does. I think, he can't be real.
He must be god, a saint, or even some minor figure from
A Bible story I forgot a long time ago. He is my savior,
Come bellying up to this bar, in this place where the wind blows
All the time off the West Bench.

How can I leave him? Should I stay and drink the whispers from his mouth?
Should I tell him how, in this sad and arid place, I've been waiting only for
Him?
That I could catch all that's left of him and turn it to a paste of spittle and
Pirate ashes?

And I know he's a drunk on a stool at a bar in a small town in Idaho. And
I know
That I'm flinging myself into the eastern wind, that low, wet mountains
Covered in trees are waiting for me, singing "come home now fool.
Your time in the desert is over."

Heart

The Occupant

What if we could light up like Christmas trees?
—heady, smug, and bright for the season—
Know protective armor as more than thin skin stretched tight over bones
The glow of a modern age might replace the fragile soul

Joint and socket, we are less than birds, more than birds.
Flightless runners running to the toilet, to the airport,
Fingers working the shuttle of reality.

      Weave it
              Take it apart
                            Wash the blood out
              Start over
And keep your fingers to yourself next time.

Another mouth flaps open, another eye blinks
Wicked center, golden iris competing for the title
"window to the soul".

Standing in line, locked up like some Penelope on a postcard
That says undo, redo, rewrite the history of your invention,
I am splayed apart, tributary of a spleen that vents without me.
Falling down is the mercury that stains the ground
And dances on its surface too,
Oiling the floorboards of my next phase.
            Try on
                  New things
                           Make them old
Discard pronouns
He
     She
          Us
Defy gravity again

Some Thoughts on the Problem of Solitude

I've recently decided I don't like quiet.
It makes me feel like those I love are already dead,
The lost friends, sad boys who are dead to me but live somewhere.
The silence on the other end of the phone when my father falters
And can't remember where Austria is or my sister's name

In the quiet, I'm one big stream of consciousness,

Like a house with all its lights on.
I bury your voice in a jar,
Jar in the yard next to the long crumbled bones of people named Clark.
It's these burdens we carry
In tiny packages that hold the weight of all that trying to be.
It makes us crack with joy and fall down hard sometimes.

Head

Moment of Truth

What would you say if I couldn't
(no wouldn't) leave it behind?
That thing I take home with me (always)
that cracking, swelling, falling-down-illusion-breaking-
congealed (like) egg yolk-mouthful-of desperation-
silent-tight-against-my-teeth moment?

It is knee-socked and frantic, swarming and fulgent.
On my desk, in the corner allocating space
      —poems tiptoe around it with monastic stealth
      —become librarians because of it.

It buzzes fugal, sonata on a cheap car stereo,
fills my head with clicks like jaw bone catches,
moves like a drunkard through the night
humming, falling, falling, humming
      —my impulse to capture that moment of truth.

What would you do if I left it with you?

Head

Poem for John Ashbery and Michael Burkard

The poet reads his poems about poets, about events and objects.
And I raise my hand and ask not about the impetus, the push,
Not about craft or line length or the sway of the ocean,

But about him, my own poetic standoff, whose lines defy
Deciphering with references aloof and sometimes off putting.
I cut my teeth on him at a time when no one knew me,
And he and I had the same kind of cluttered mind, thinky syntax,
Allusions to the long dead and never touched. But then we changed
And came into our poems, our presence less hostile, more inviting

The sea sways
        The trees are greening here, but
                I still don't walk the dog every day
I'm a cipher—code for the place
        Where the rubber hits the road
                Where flesh is still and still flesh
Oh, how the mind plays tricks on us.

Head

Ginsberg and Eliot Look Down on Robert Hass Reading "Privilege of Being"

Robert Hass is reading about illiterate angels. He looks
comfortable and middle class and very happy to be
perched on that stool at that microphone in front of
those middle class college students, who close their eyes and

let themselves linger on the word 'come.' Above, the
real angels dispute the necessity for such a show
of the earthbound in art. Ginsberg, gesturing wildly, hanging
on to his yarmulka, says: "You gotta say 'fuck' Bob, that's what

gives a poem substance, "'come' just doesn't do it: too subtle,
too middle aged." But Eliot disagrees, says "words like that
are best avoided, or cloaked in allusions to the Sutra, or
sandwiched in metaphysical conceits, like sucking fleas."

But now Hass is reading the one about the fish simmering
with the oranges (oranges!?) in the pan, and how he's loved,
and Allen and Thomas can at least agree on this one thing—
that we were all fish once, before we lost our wings.

This Is Not a Poem about Icarus

As if he didn't fly toward that sun when the sky was sliced in two,
Choosing instead to turn north toward colder climes, whereupon
His wax and feathers froze and Odin spoke saying "all curious boys
Commend themselves to wrong turns sometimes, but you flew
Right and straight this time, handing off the burdens of avarice and
Infamy." Icarus, not knowing what to say really, surveyed the heights
To which he had aspired. He counted one: I am going to cast out all
My hopes of warmth, and two: freedom's just another word for
Nothin' left to lose. The song ringing true in his head, Icarus looked up
And saw his blood blue number written on the sky. "When I am 33"
He said, "I will die then and all the world will love me."

Head

Staring Contest: For Herodotus

Herodotus, I heard he died writing about fingers, and so
I swear I'll never fall asleep with a pen in my hand
To wake up and record my dreams for history.
That short, full word's an enemy written on my eyebrow sometimes,
Lost and sad like summer ice that melts too fast.

The journeys of the old and dead are what interest me
That turning away from my preoccupation
With the rise and fall of your gaze
And the contest of who'll blink first.
And deine augenblick will be my victory in our old worn out battle.

Herodotus, his reputation on the line in exile,
looked to the horizon, past the smell of olives and the sound of Sirens.

The Highway Girl

She's there on the side of the highway
on long trips that smell like winter car and truck stop coffee.
She's the tattered plastic bag flapping in the median,
destination nowhere, cigarette stream from the car in front of me,
festive almost, but soon extinguished.
She's a bride.

She's the absolute meaning of the word careen—reckless and soothing,
floating from some vapor trail of thought. And she tells me "look"
when my eyes should be on the road. In snowdrifts
she reclines and entices me with the thought that there's more to life
than just staying in the lines.
She's bad like that.

She's a woman born of all my thoughts of straying, and she lives
in sideways glances and unfinished departures.
She's an eyeblink, the wantonness in driving home so late,
the swerving inside my head as I grab the wheel and steady myself for
another mile.

Head

The Capital of Me

In my fifties will I
Raisin?
Become a piece
Of leather meat?
Lose my tender
To chewiness?

In dreams my face
Settles into a map
Or some such
Paltry metaphor

From what I've seen
The capital of me is small
That red spot on my belly
Bright and slightly raised
That calls attention to
The blood underneath.

Home

Five Years On: Clinton, NY 2008

I live in a village with a clock tower
That sounds like spittle in the winter.
I live next door to a fireman
Whose brother-in-law
Watches cartoons at fifty-eight,
Takes a short bus to the city,
And sorts pins from nails,
Nails from bolts another lines up boxes for.

I live in lake effect some days,
When wide white bands blow
Through Onondaga, take its claim of steel gone away,
And the wreckage of steel gone away to be fired
In other cities with unpronounceable names.

We're the grey behind the fuse light,
Spent and done, demented in our wool caps,
Eating dinner in our coats. We're all that's left
When walk time hovers near the edge of restraint.
How brave we are, how cold our fingers waiting
For the coming of another spring

Home

English Teacher

On the chalkboard my writing goes downhill on those days when all I want is to stay home or turn to greet their faces, some downcast, some sullen, some expectant, and say "I'm a goddamn poet you know."

I should be somewhere watching birds and writing bird poems.
I anticipate my own flight into words,
into images that streak through stanzas
and defy the moments of "I don't have anything to say anymore."

I am not dried up!!! My flight from mountain desert took care of that. I'm waterlogged; if anything the rain has made me feel my feet more than I used to.

Spring means everything greens here and smells like a cross between dirt and armpits, not warm enough to smell like tar yet, but not frozen anymore. We're in limbo here, no real leaves on the trees, but skunks are coming out to add their scent to the catalog of smelled but not seen.

Mornings, I sit on the back porch with cigarettes,
smoke and phlegm rising with the sun.
Birds are replacing my snowplow alarm clock,
and I don't drive to work in the dark anymore

almanac: Syracuse NY and Seattle WA have the least sun of any two cities in the lower forty-eight, nine, whatever, states. At least there's always something to do in Seattle, but you have to dress in black to do it. Syracuse is wind from the lake and a downtown that's closed on Saturday afternoons. Seattle is mid-winter Smiths covers at the Crocodile Cafe

Compare the places you don't love and you might love the place you're in. That's the logic of poetry, I suppose.

There's a place in my backyard that rises delicately like a grave
and the foundation of a carriage house.

Home

history: this whole town's on an Indian burial site and the cemetery rots
with revolutionary war heroes.
I am only the third family to own this old house,
the first to paint a room inside it red.
It's a hard place to leave on days when I just want to scream that I'm a poet.

Home

On the E Train

On the subway great necked men bend
over their sandwiches, read the Koran,
make the train a house of prayer
while three rails hum beneath us.

This city's delinquent steam, a wreck pulled
out of itself. Uphill in only occasional ways,
it slides not much from cable onto drip coated pylon,
breaks the backs of the men who make it shine.

Jesus in miniature hangs everywhere, buffed glossy
with the love of old ladies' rubbings
in salted bodegas on the edge of the park.

This city's absurdly tilted, disheveled: it's a fire sale
fed when the members of a hundred stunted
alphabets come and go daily, and then it's easy to ride under water.

Home

Earthquake

And when the ground grew shaky and things fell off shelves
In small bodegas and public libraries, all the same way
Cartons of cigarettes and imprints of Keats, soda spurting and
Eliot's argument about the metaphysicals, all the same way.
Products fell off the shelves, false icons that promise
Look younger, quit smoking, shed inches, he will love you.

When the streets, filled with the litter of all our making,
Heaved up like a stomach almost, like wind from the mouth
We hid in bathtubs, basements. Wait, it was not a tornado!
Some welcomed another coming because who but god himself
Could make the ground split, cut a rift with edges jagged,
A crooked smile beautiful when seen from space.

I walked along a great rift once. It bore that name even.
It seemed the desert had said "go ahead. I'll bear those gashes
And never say anything, never cause a stir." Maybe
That's the way it is sometimes when the land gets put in its place.
If I said we're like that scar
In that big desert you would laugh at my bad simile.
An earthquake, a hurricane, a tornado, it's all the same really.

Home

Saratoga Springs in the Off-season

Saturday
Downtown, the Adelphi Hotel is empty: a vacant unreadable Araby.
Crisp white sheets cover Queen Annes that sit like brides waiting to be unveiled.
Only their wings can be seen, flightless in winter—
emptiness to be roosted in by summer tourists
who come for the track and the shops.

Sunday
On the outskirts of town snow still tenants the dim places between birches and pines,
lingers into April like a lover too scared to tiptoe to his car in the middle of the night,
who knows that staying only makes it worse sometimes, like loitering snow keeps the ground colder longer.

Monday
A nor'easter blows down Broadway,
peppering eyes with the leftovers of street salt—
traction when winter was really here: now eyeball grit.
The Celtic pub swells with every U2 and Van Morrison song
imaginable, and over the din I hear everyone's stories of THE WEST.
Roger went from Rutgers to BYU because it was a cheap western adventure.
Sally had to take four planes to get from Albany to Sun Valley once for a ski trip.
When the small talk is over, Arlene tells me that three days before she married she fell out of love.

Tuesday...
is flight day. Albany to Cincinnati: Cincinnati to Salt Lake.
I watch as a returning Mormon missionary clips his nails reverently:
He will herald my return to birchlessness.
The woman next to me is large and nervous, fans herself with a magazine and sighs frequently.

Home

Across the aisle an asthmatic begins his ritual of inhalers, lining them up on the lap tray
as he prepares to spend three hours in a world of other people's exhalations. Flying into Salt Lake City is like slipping between the sheets, but the sheets are cold, and dark, and rock as I return to the smooth speech of mountain terrain.

Home

Bird Watching In Central New York

One: Is when I get out my binoculars
To zoom in on a cardinal
Eating in a snowless patch
Of my backyard, small dart,
Red and determined to graze.
He's gone in an instant.
It's March; when the hell
Will the birds come back?

  Two: Is when I put on my facebook page
Me + binoculars = your thoughts?
My friends respond: birdwatcher, sniper,
Paranoid. I don't get the last one.

   Three: It's the butt crack of dawn, and
I am looking for deer, moving
Through my yard and back to the woods,
Silent and graceful like small ships,
But I see none.
I imagine seeing someone at the edge
Of my property looking at me, or worse,
Looking at me through binoculars.

    Four: The yard is less snow, more grass now.
I am reinventing myself with spring
Into a birdwatcher, deer watcher, crocheter
Of long and apparently endless chains
Because I cannot turn and stitch.
I am calming myself with tasks that
Require patience.

Home

    Five: I have thrown my chain in the bedside table
And twice across the room. I've cut two
Lengths for the cat to play with. The scarf
I predicted would be soothing and a Christmas gift
For my love might be done by February, if ever.

    Six: There is danger in promising gifts
That signify creation, that require more than love.

Home

On Vacation in Cape Cod I think of Idaho, Home, and Other Places

In Idaho they're breathing smoke right now. The desert, crying "burn baby burn" gives up outbuildings, sagebrush, condominiums and homes. Here, we can't imagine fire taking hold. The rain comes smelling like chlorine afterwards, and while it's on there may be a flash flood, or someone may find Jesus again. What can I do? The people are nice, they smile, say hello, and mow their own lawns. Sometimes it's all too much.

Because I'm from New Jersey, and there at 7:45 the lawn crews start their engines. I gripe and think about who I might call to put a turd in their $6.00-an-hour life so my father can sleep in. At 97 he has little else to do but stay in bed and dream about the city, the boat, the war, his long dead family.

In upstate New York we're soggy and feed on greens and riggies, pronounce certain words as if they've been lying in the back of our throats for a while. The rains wash our trees, and we know no tan, no brown in summer, no sun in winter. Delirium too energetic, we dig our cars out schloggy, hoisting and dumping the lake effect to piles on each side of the driveway. My snow's as high as me some years, and I am hid behind it, easy to be wan and gray as the shortest of days.

In Idaho on a big sky day, you can see the top of Chink's Peak, and the gap and the cows aren't dusted. Miles away the Tetons rise like jagged teeth and meth is cooked in their shadows. Mormons look south to where Mahroni and his horn stand proud, and the rest of us just look up and pray for rain.

Home

We All Go A'looking

1.
My friend has been, not arrested, no, but
the police want to know about the footprints
in the wet, clayless mud that led to her window.
He said the cat had wandered, really it was all
a misunderstanding, an overreaction from a 15
year old girl, who saw, or thought she saw, the tips
of his curly red hair.

2.
Sometimes I walk the dog after dark, and I look
at people's window treatments, furniture, how they
combine past and present in this town of big,
old houses. I do not want to see them fight, fuck,
eat dinner or do anything personal. Do not want
to hear what they are playing on their stereos or
what they're watching on tv.

3.
My sister and I are walking in New Jersey,
where neither of us lives but both of us grew up.
We have different accents but the same need
to look at living rooms, kitchens, and the occasional
bedroom after dark. From the sidewalk (This is very
important you understand. We don't go into yards)
we see a swag that frames perfectly the large lamp
it surrounds, all suburban symmetry.

4.
If we really saw something I think the night
would be ruined, the veil lifted in a way that might
flood the lawn with motion sensor starkness, give
too much reality to it all: our parents fading by larger
and larger degrees. The work it takes to keep it all in place.
These aren't the things we want to know.

Home

One Morning

As the fog sat low in my backyard
Two deer returning from their night jobs
Came through the trees
Quiet at first but then
They stopped to play near where
The apple trees used to be.
They chased and bucked
As if they had no other purpose
Then receded into the woods.
I heard them noisy then
Crashing, not caring that the birds
Fled their perches, heard the wake
Of them as they ran through one yard,
Another. I listened 'til they were gone.

Then came away to write this poem
As if I had some purpose,
As if words could do anything
To compare to those brief moments
When the deer were playing in my yard.

Home

Leaving Idaho Behind

"Who r u?" the caterpillar said
and I had no answer

I told him the specifics:
my mouth is chalk
my teeth are cracking
my flight is leaving

I am a picture in his scrapbook
scrapbook in a box
box in a closet
closet down the hallway
I am here, and
when the snow falls
in wide, white bands
I curse the sky and the groundhog

Spring will be late this year
the farmers need the water
the aquifer is drying
potato, potato, potato

I work for a living too
generate paper, say smart things
wait for summer, hide underground
and try not to fall again

Home

Winterish

As winter settled itself into winter
we cut ourselves in two,
into two, into two ones.
It has
the burning of an exorcism,
the jaggedness of shattered glass,
the aching of an unbirth and
all the false solace of a pile of ashes.

When the streets were ice packed
and dreams were dirtied,
people hid behind their turned up collars,
muffled cold air with scarves and
those robbery hats, and in a bar
down by the railroad tracks
I told a stranger the story of us.

The ripping didn't start 'til later
when I drove home past the shutdown town
cursing Mormons and the nuclear family unit
and smug, snug houses and chanting
"car, take me where you want to go".

Home

Not on My Life

From outside I could tell the birds were back
And when I woke up my fingers were in my mouth.
You said it's like each moment leaning into the next, and
I started a catalog of all the things that passed between us.

1) The sky didn't come back big.
2) I didn't miss my flight
3) The cat never lapped anything fallen or spilled
4) There was no cat, no sky
No resurrected syntax.
Just the smell of the Atlantic in my feet

One night I stood blowing smoke at an Idaho sky,
My cracked window its thoughtful swelling border
And learned that metal comes from all of us
Who know the rock and the hard place

Home

When I Went Back to Idaho—for Catherine

On the side of the I-15, I swear there were forty deer
Standing in the fog just past Malad Summit,
Coming down from the mountain for a false spring.

At the rest stop the turnoff to Lava Hot Springs
Went there without me that time. I was on my way
To another place, but I stopped and looked up
That road past the swimming hole that goes to
The hot pools at the old hotel and the ice cream
Store and the candy store with the sign that says
"We do not sell ice cream!"

The roads here are free, freewheeling through sagebrush
And in Idaho you never have to pay a toll. The names
Of dead Indians, Mormons, and shiny minerals signify
Towns you pass by, not through. In Pocatello there
Is wind and people who remember me.

Home for me is a funny thing. My home has Indian names too,
Onondaga, Oneida, and the like, but my roads are narrower and wind
Around the curves of low mountains full of trees.

After dark on the Brimfield Road, the car lights keep deer in the fields
Most of the time, but on the thruway I pay to see them alive or
Dead on the side of the road sometimes. It's the life I thought would turn
To gold the obsidian I left behind.

The car will start today and head east, the dog will almost die again
From so much excitement. Tonight I'll eat steak and you'll eat fish in a place as old
As Puritans and Indians, and we'll wonder at how we got here to these places
Named by the long dead and left to us.

Home

Springtime in Central New York

Sometimes it rains in blood blue sheets, sometimes water
Careening down my street picks up the jetsam but not
The flotsam. Sometimes it rains a hungry-eyed way, with
Water searching out every opportunity to fill, soak, pervade,
And sometimes it's the smell of too much rain that sponges up
My lawn and all the fabric of my little world. I am full and bloated,
The worm that rises to the sidewalk, left without my raft,
Without my lifejacket.

When the sun does come, its light is stillborn and soon gone.
Heat rising like an errant lover doesn't last long and all the bonfires
Get lit at night when bats come out to flit and glide from tree
To house. Light the lamp, call the dog, I am done with the days
Of all my sorrows. Done with the waiting and the worry
Of finger chewing madness. Spring will come someday and
End another winter of this grey malaise. Spring will push me out
And into whatever it has in store for me.

Patricia Murphy earned masters and doctoral degrees in English from Idaho State University. Originally from New Jersey, she lived in Idaho for over twenty years. She now resides in Central New York, where she teaches writing and Interdisciplinary Studies at the State University of New York Polytechnic Institute. *CityArt, Arsenic Lobster, River Walk Literary Journal, Breadcrumb Scabs, Yes, Poetry,* and *Adagio Verse* have published her poetry and fiction.